# The Talker

By Sunita Apte and Genuine Pyun
Illustrated by Kate McKeon

Scott Foresman
is an imprint of

PEARSON

Glenview, Illinois • Boston, Massachusetts • Chandler, Arizona •
Upper Saddle River, New Jersey

**Illustrations**
Kate McKeon.

**Photographs**

Every effort has been made to secure permission and provide appropriate credit for photographic material. The publisher deeply regrets any omission and pledges to correct errors called to its attention in subsequent editions.

Unless otherwise acknowledged, all photographs are the property of Pearson Education, Inc.

**19** Joe Rosenthal/©AP Images.

ISBN 13: 978-0-328-52149-4
ISBN 10: 0-328-52149-3

2 3 4 5 6 7 8 9 10 V0N4 13 12 11 10

# Table of Contents

# Chapter 1: Boarding School

Joe burrowed deeper under the covers of his cot. Lights out at his boarding school had come an hour ago, but he still couldn't sleep. He was restless and he hated the way the cot and the covers felt. He wished he were back at home on the Reservation, sleeping in his family's hogan under a blanket his mother had woven.

Joe missed his family and his life back home terribly. He didn't dare let anyone else see how homesick he was, though. Joe had seen other students punished for saying they missed their homes, and he didn't want to risk receiving a punishment by telling someone who might not be trustworthy how he felt.

Joe had been at the boarding school in Shiprock, New Mexico, for almost a year now, but he still hadn't grown accustomed to it. There were so many rules and restrictions, the place seemed more like a jail than a school. The boys were punished if they spoke Navajo instead of English, punished if they didn't keep their hair short, punished if their uniforms weren't just right.

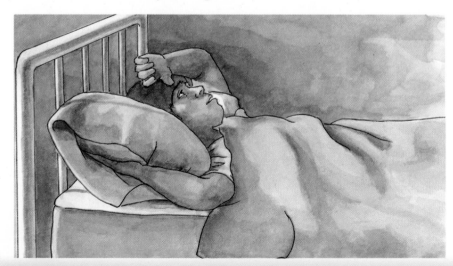

Joe's grandmother only spoke Navajo, and he was afraid if he stopped speaking it, he'd forget the language. How would he be able to talk to her? And if they couldn't communicate, how could their relationship remain close? So in order to ensure that he never forgot, he murmured to himself in Navajo late at night, when no one could hear.

In fact, "Joe" wasn't even his real name! The people at the school had forced him to change it to seem "more American."

"You will be Joe now," he recalled his teacher stating. "You'll be an American now."

Joe longed for the freedom and sunlight of the reservation and for the long unhurried days spent on horseback with his father. He longed for quiet evenings back home, with his aunt working on the silver and turquoise jewelry she artfully crafted, and the clickety-clack of his mother's loom breaking the evening silence. He longed for the vibrant red rocks and purple hills of the countryside, not the drab, gray sameness that came with living in a town.

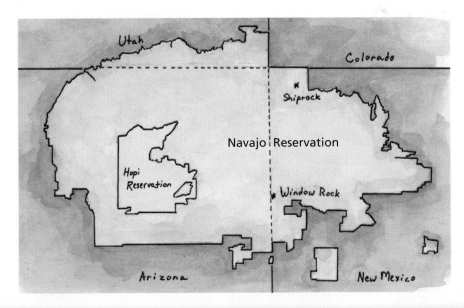

His teacher repeatedly reminded him how fortunate he was to be at school, that he should be gracious and honored that they would teach him to be civilized. Joe always had to swallow his pride and hold down his anger and frustration toward such offensive statements. He didn't understand what was so uncivilized about his life on the reservation.

Still, he reluctantly had to admit that he *was* lucky to be getting an education. It was 1942, there was a war going on, and life was hard for everyone. Just being provided a school to attend was fortuitous when the majority of the country's attention and energy was on the war. The war had spread from Europe to Asia, and young men around the country were sprinting to get in on the action.

Even Navajo men were joining the army. Just yesterday, Joe's friend Sam had told him that the Marines were looking for Navajo soldiers. His thoughts floated back to that conversation.

"Where have you been all day, Sam?" Joe asked inquisitively.

"Around—I heard some of the other guys in our class talking about enlisting today after class, and so I went down to the recruitment center to check it out," responded Sam, thoughtfully.

"Are you going to sign up?" Joe asked.

"I don't know," Sam sighed, as he kicked at the dusty ground. As he watched the dust rise from the earth, he lifted his gaze probingly to his friend. In a determined voice, he boldly asserted, "I will if you'll come with me! Life in the Marines can't be any worse than this school, can it?"

Joe hesitated, thoughtfully. "No—I guess not," he conceded slowly. "But I'll need time to think about it."

And so here he was, a night later, unable to sleep and thinking about his future. Joe always dreamed of going back to the reservation, working the land, and helping his father herd their flock of sheep. But now he was presented with an intriguing, and yet frightening, opportunity—he could join the Marines and possibly see some remote places that he could hardly imagine visiting if he ever traveled on his own.

He was torn in two directions. It wasn't just that he was homesick and wanted to return to the reservation. Deep in his heart, he believed in the importance of making sacrifices for his country. But it wasn't as simple as that.

The main issue was, did he want to fight for a government that didn't even allow him, or any other Navajo, to vote? There was a grim irony in the situation—he could lose his life for the democracy of the United States, and yet his parents still wouldn't be permitted to vote for the nation's next president.

All the military recruiters emphasized the importance to fight for America's freedom. But Joe often wondered, *What about my own people's freedom?* All of the people who were asking him to fight for America, weren't they the descendants of the people who took Navajo lands and forced his people to live on reservations? Where was the freedom in that?

His grandma had told him stories about a tragic event called The Long Walk. Members of the Navajo nation had been forced to walk almost 300 miles to be held captive in a fort. When they were finally released, the only way to get home was to walk the entire way back. Thousands had died by the time everyone was back on the reservation, she told him.

She said they had even killed the Navajo's livestock and burned their fields to persuade them to surrender. He wondered why he should fight for a country that would do this to his people. Of course, he knew this was a long time ago and wanted to believe that things had changed. It was all very confusing.

# Chapter 2: In Training

After a week of wrestling with his thoughts, Joe finally made up his mind. He knew what was the right thing to do. He couldn't change the past, but he could help pave a new future for the country. Americans had so much potential to learn from different cultures and grow in understanding.

Joe and Sam walked to the recruitment station to enlist in the Marines. The Marine there seemed unusually pleased to see them.

"Can you read and write in English?" he inquired.

Joe and Sam exchanged a glance. Why would he need to know that? Soldiers didn't read or write— they fought.

Sam cleared his throat. "Joe can read and write very well in English," he said. "I can, too, but Joe is better."

Joe's face flushed slightly with embarrassment. It was true that he was a good student. His English teacher always praised him, particularly about his writing. Still, it made him uncomfortable to be complimented.

The Marine wrote a special note in their files about their education. He signed them up and told them to report for duty the following week.

When they arrived, they found the training camp in San Diego to be grueling but predictable. It was tough physical work, which Joe had anticipated, but he didn't mind the effort it required. He had always worked hard at home, helping his dad with chores on the farm such as herding the sheep and shearing their wool. He wasn't afraid of manual labor.

To Joe's surprise, after training camp, he and Sam didn't prepare to depart with the rest of the recruits. Instead, they were sent to Camp Pendleton for additional training to be part of a top-secret program! There they discovered why the marine recruiter had been so interested in their education. They needed to be able to read and write because they were going to be code talkers, or messengers. They would use the Navajo language to send secret messages over the radio that the enemy couldn't decode.

Joe couldn't believe it! After teachers at his school had spent months and months forbidding him to speak his Navajo language, now the American government wanted him to use it to aid the military! The teachers had told him he'd be better off just to forget the language—that English was all he needed to know. But it was lucky for them that he'd kept speaking it in bed at night. They'd really be up a creek if he'd forgotten it!

At Camp Pendleton, they attended a special eight-week messenger-training course. Besides Joe and Sam, there were about 30 other Navajo in the program. Joe knew quite a few of them, some from the school in Shiprock and others from the reservation.

The young men spent their days in the classroom, learning to create a code and use it to send messages quickly. They developed Navajo code words for many military terms. For example, a fighter plane became a *da-ha-tih-hi*, or "hummingbird," and a dive-bomber became a *gini*, or "chicken hawk." A battleship was a *lo-tso*, or "whale." They also came up with Navajo words that would represent letters in the English alphabet. For instance, *wol-la-chee* (ant) and *be-la-sana* (apple) could both stand for the letter *A*.

Joe thought it was interesting, like working on a puzzle. He was only sad that he couldn't tell his family back home about the exciting and vital work he was doing for the United States. Every code talker was sworn to absolute secrecy. If the enemy broke the code, they could learn important information that would help them prepare for battle. That would mean more American lives could be lost unnecessarily, and so no one could know what these young Navajo men were doing. Even when they left the Marine Corps, they weren't permitted to talk about or even mention Code Talking.

Joe, Sam, and the others worked day after day for weeks, until they knew the code so well they could use it in their sleep. They could send and decode complicated messages in just a few minutes. This was a huge improvement from the code system the military normally used. They were told that under the old system, it would sometimes take hours to decode a message!

# Chapter 3: At War

Finally, the time had come to ship out. Joe was in the barracks one afternoon, cleaning up, when Sam came sprinting in.

"Guess what!" he cried breathlessly. "We're shipping out to the Pacific to fight the Japanese. We're finally going to see some action!"

Going to the Pacific? Joe couldn't believe it. It was exciting, but also a little frightening. He still had so many questions. Were the code talkers all going to be assigned to different battalions and companies? Or would he be going alone? He was nervous at the thought of being the only Navajo in his company. Joe knew that some Americans still didn't trust the people they called Indians. If there were no other Navajo around him, Joe feared he would feel more lonely and homesick than he had been at his boarding school.

Sam must have read his thoughts. He smiled mischievously at Joe. "Can you believe they assigned us to the same company?" he asked, his face breaking out into a lopsided grin. "I guess I'll have to find a way to put up with you for a few more months!"

A few months slowly turned into a couple of years. Finally, in February of 1945, Joe and Sam found themselves on the Pacific island of Iwo Jima. It was in a location that was vital to both American and Japanese military strategies. Twenty thousand Japanese soldiers were protecting the island, and they weren't about to give it up. The Marine Corps would have to take it from them.

As usual, Joe and Sam were busy relaying messages. Many different divisions were involved in the attack on Iwo Jima, so a lot of top-secret communication was necessary. Even a few years into his job, Joe was amazed at the system of Navajo words they had developed. Their code had not been broken by the Japanese, and it didn't look as though it ever would be.

Though he liked the Marines, Joe missed home fiercely. The reservation was thousands of miles away—so far that it might as well have been on another planet. Sometimes, lying in his tent at night, he closed his eyes and pretended he was sleeping under the desert stars, with a cool night breeze gently licking his face. He pictured his mother, father, aunt, and grandmother sitting down to dinner and talking about their days.

Joe longed to be with his family, but he knew that at the moment what he was doing was more important. If the United States could win the war, he would see them soon enough. And every message he successfully sent or received put them one step closer to a victory for all Americans, even the Navajo in his reservation.

However, sometimes it was hard to keep all that in mind. So many of the other Marines were suspicious of him and didn't always make him feel comfortable or welcome. Thank goodness Sam was around!

One night, Joe looked up from his work to see Sam being marched back to camp by two armed soldiers from another company.

"We found this Japanese soldier wearing an American uniform," one of them told Bill, the camp sentry. "We think he might be a spy."

"I told you guys, I'm an American soldier," Sam repeated for what must have been the umpteenth time. "I'm not Japanese, I'm Navajo. I'm from New Mexico."

Joe leapt up to rescue his friend, but Bill got there first. The sentry was a friend of theirs and knew Sam well.

"That's no Japanese soldier; that's Sam!" he told the soldiers from the other company. "He's one of our communications guys. He's Navajo. Let him be!"

Joe stepped forward into the light from Bill's lantern. Maybe it would help if they saw another soldier with brown skin and straight black hair. The soldiers from the other company looked dubiously from Sam to Bill to Joe. Then one of them prodded Sam in the back.

"Go on then," he muttered. "Sorry for the mistake."

As the three friends watched the soldiers leave, Sam whispered, "I tell you, it's dangerous out there!" Sam was trying to make light of it, but Joe could see that his friend was shaken up.

It was incredibly unfair. Their job on Iwo Jima was dangerous enough without having to prove that they were American on top of it. They already had to worry about defending themselves against the Japanese, but now it was evident that they had to worry about their safety while they were inside their own camp too!

While some soldiers had shifted their prejudiced views and showed more acceptance and friendship, it was not a universal sentiment. The Navajo men had thought that their participation in the war would bring about trust and recognition from their fellow Americans, but it would take much longer than they realized—37 years longer!

A few days after the incident, Joe and Sam ran into Ira Hayes, a member of the Pima nation from Arizona. Ira was with a different company, and he was a regular soldier, not a code talker. Though he had made a number of friends among his company, he had quickly developed a friendship with Joe and Sam and loved to chat whenever he saw them.

"Hey, did you hear about us raising the flag on Mount Suribachi?" he asked proudly.

Joe nodded his head. Everyone had heard about it. Mount Suribachi was one of the biggest hills on the island and one of the Japanese strongholds on Iwo Jima. It had been a big event when the Americans had finally captured it. A photographer had snapped a picture that had been in all the papers back home.

"Yeah, your company is famous now," Joe said. "Those guys who raised the flag really earned some glory."

Ira smiled at him. "Well, I was one of those guys."

Joe couldn't believe it. Ira had been one of the soldiers to raise the flag? He was happy for his friend, but he couldn't help thinking about how different their homecomings would be. Ira would return home a hero, but Joe was forbidden to tell anyone about being a code talker. It didn't seem just that he had to keep such an exceptional secret.

Joe wished he could have his picture in the newspaper. He longed to be able to show his family and friends some evidence of the crucial role he had played for the Marines. Secretly, he wanted to shout to the world that his beloved Navajo language was helping the United States win the war. It was hard to keep this contained inside. Still, if it helped his country win the war, then he could live with it—he knew he *must* live with it.

## Chapter 4: Going Home

Finally, after a battle that lasted most of February and March of 1945, U.S. forces captured the entire island of Iwo Jima. All of the Code Talkers had worked around the clock in their efforts to encode and decode messages for their company to reach this victory, and the effort paid off.

At last, it was time for Joe and Sam's company to head home. One day during one of his final shifts at the communications station, Joe received the message that the time had finally arrived. This time, it was his turn to go bolting to Sam with good news.

"Guess what?!" he shouted. And without giving Sam a chance to guess, blurted out, "We're going home!"

Sam didn't believe him initially. They both missed the reservation more than they cared to admit. The longing to go home had been overwhelming to the point of being painful. And now the thought of going home and seeing their families again was almost too much to bear.

Sam poked Joe in the shoulder. "What's the first thing you're going to do when you get home?" he asked.

Joe thought about it for a moment. "I'm going to ride a horse into the hills around my house. Then I'm going to spend an afternoon leaning against a rock in the hot sun, watching my flock of *dibeh*, my sheep. After that, I'm going to sit and talk to my family for hours in Navajo, but for once, none of it will be a code or for anyone else to hear!"

Sam grinned. "Me, the first thing I'm going to do is ask my mother to cook three dinners for me."

Joe laughed. Sam was always hungry. His thoughts of home went straight through his stomach. Joe had to admit, though, that a home-cooked meal sounded amazing. Even with all the places he'd been, Joe still felt that no food on Earth was better than his mother's homemade fry bread.

His mouth started to water at the thought of it. For so long, he tried not to think about all the things he missed back home, but now that they were leaving, his memories came flooding back.

21

Joe realized he missed the fry bread so much that he thought he might eat nothing but fry bread for the rest of his life! Of course, he knew his mother would probably make him a huge meal with all of his favorites, not just fry bread, and that would be just fine too.

Joe sat back on his cot and pictured his mother, standing in the doorway of their hogan, her eyes squinting in the sunlight as he hugged her. Later, after a big meal, they would sit outside in the violet evening light as she talked to him about the war.

"What did you do over there, Son?" his mother would ask.

Joe closed his eyes, thinking of all the things he would want to say but wouldn't be able to. What could he tell her that was even close to the truth? He wanted to be as honest as possible.

Joe went over it all again and again in his mind, discarding all sorts of possibilities, until finally he realized that the best answer was the truth. When his mother asked him what he did, he would simply answer:

*"I talked."*

# The Navajo Code Talkers

More than 400 Navajo men became code talkers in the Pacific during World War II. The idea began with Philip Johnston, an American who had grown up on the Navajo Reservation. Johnston convinced the military that the Navajo, whose complex language was spoken by only a handful of outsiders, would make good code talkers. Soon, the first group of 29 code talkers was recruited, with hundreds more trained later.

The code talkers' contribution to the United States victory in the Pacific was enormous. In fact, one marine major on Iwo Jima stated, "Were it not for the Navajos, the marines would never have taken the island."

Despite their important role, the code talkers were sworn to secrecy and received no official recognition when they initially returned home. It wasn't until 1968 that the military even acknowledged them. Finally, the Navajo Code Talkers were officially recognized in 1982, 37 years after their victory in Iwo Jima, when President Ronald Reagan declared August 14 National Code Talkers Day.

In 2000 Congress passed the Honoring the Code Talkers Act. And in 2001, the first group of 29 code talkers received the Congressional Gold Medal and 400 others received the Congressional Silver Medal. At long last, in 2008, a monument to the code talkers was erected in Phoenix, Arizona.